LOVE & LIFE

A PERSONAL MEMOIR
THE LIGHT THAT LINGERS

Atosha Logan

LOVE & LIFE

A PERSONAL MEMOIR
THE LIGHT THAT LINGERS

Atosha Logan

COPYRIGHT © 2025 BY ATOSHA LOGAN

ALL RIGHTS RESERVED. NO PART OF THIS PUBLICATION MAY BE REPRODUCED, DISTRIBUTED, OR TRANSMITTED IN ANY FORM OR BY ANY MEANS, INCLUDING PHOTOCOPYING, RECORDING, OR OTHER ELECTRONIC OR MECHANICAL METHODS, OR OTHERWISE WITHOUT THE PRIOR WRITTEN PERMISSION OF THE AUTHOR, EXCEPT IN THE CASE OF BRIEF QUOTATIONS EMBODIED IN REVIEWS, ARTICLES, OR CRITICAL WORKS.

PLEASE NOTE THAT NO PART OF THIS BOOK MAY BE USED OR REPRODUCED IN ANY MANNER FOR THE PURPOSE OF TRAINING, ARTIFICIAL INTELLIGENCE TECHNOLOGIES, OR SYSTEMS.

FOR PERMISSION REQUESTS, CONTACT THE AUTHOR AT:
ATOSHA LOGAN, AUTHOR & PUBLISHER
INFO@ATOSHALOGAN.COM
WWW.ATOSHALOGAN.COM

ISBN: 978-1-7362267-2-8 (PAPERBACK) 978-1-7362267-3-5 (E-BOOK)
FIRST EDITION

PRINTED IN THE UNITED STATES OF AMERICA

COVER DESIGN: ATOSHA LOGAN
INTERIOR LAYOUT: ATOSHA LOGAN

About the Author

Atosha Logan is a woman of faith, strength, and purpose who has dedicated more than two decades to the field of education and is an author, certified life coach, and consultant. Guided by her unwavering belief in God, she has poured her heart into nurturing, mentoring, and leading others with integrity and personal motivation. Her journey reflects resilience, hope, and a deep commitment to uplifting and empowering others.

Beyond her professional calling, Atosha treasures the bonds of family and the importance of legacy. She believes that life's experiences are not only meant to be lived but also shared as testimonies of God's grace. Her passion for legacy and storytelling is rooted in a belief that God's grace carries us through every season. This memoir is her gift of love, hope, and inspiration for generations to come.

She continues to live out her purpose with faith at the center, striving to leave behind a legacy of inspiration, love, and unwavering trust in God.

Atosha Logan

info@atoshalogan.com
www.atoshalogan.com

ACKNOWLEDGEMENTS

This memoir is the reflection of many hearts and hands that have touched my life, and I am deeply grateful for each one.

God has BLESSED me with a wonderful husband and three children!

To my family—you are my foundation and my greatest source of love and support. Thank you for standing beside me through every season of joy and trial, and for reminding me daily of the meaning of unconditional love. I am grateful for the wisdom you've shared and the lessons that continue to guide my journey. Each of you has left an imprint on my story that cannot be erased.

To my close friends, thank you for your laughter, encouragement, and honesty. Your presence has been a light in both the brightest and darkest moments, and your belief in me gave me the courage to keep writing.

Most of all, I give thanks to God. Without His grace, strength, and faithfulness, none of this would have been possible. Every chapter of my life is a testament to His unfailing love.

The Legacy of Jerald & Willie Mae Williams shall continue through me!
A Legacy to Live For Inc.

THE LIGHT THAT LINGERS

This *Personal Memoir* belongs to:

_____

DATE:

A Personal Memoir of Life & Love

Personal Memoir
Introduction

Every life is a story, and this one unfolds through moments of triumph, heartbreak, resilience, and hope. This memoir invites readers into an intimate journey, walking beside the author through seasons of growth, reflection, and discovery. It is a narrative that celebrates the power of memory, the strength of the human spirit, and the beauty of living fully.

From the roots that anchor us to the branches that stretch toward new horizons, these pages capture both struggle and victory. Each memory serves as a reminder that while we cannot control every circumstance, we can shape the legacy we leave behind.

This memoir is more than a story—it's an invitation to reflect on your own journey, to honor the memories that shape you, and to be inspired to live with courage and hope. reminding you of where you've been, who has walked beside you, and the dreams still waiting ahead.

Open these pages, take part in the journey, and let it spark reflection, conversation, and connection in your own life with grace, gratitude, and courage.

PERSONAL MEMOIR
Table of Content

ALL ABOUT ME (11)

FAMILY TREE (14)

IDENTITY & ROOTS (17)

CHILDHOOD & COMING OF AGE (32)

FAMILY & RELATIONSHIPS (46)

EDUCATION, WORK & PURPOSE (61)

HOME, PLACES & BELONGING (76)

TRADITION, CULTURE & CELEBRATION (88)

CHALLENGES & RESILIENCE (101)

JOY, PASSIONS & HOBBIES (115)

FAITH, VALUES & PHILOSOPHY (127)

LEGACY & HOPES (139)

LIFE'S REFLECTIONS (153)

LETTER(S) TO LOVE ONE (154)

A PERSONAL MEMOIR OF LIFE & LOVE

"BE YOURSELF; EVERYONE ELSE IS ALREADY TAKEN."
— OSCAR WILDE

A PERSONAL MEMOIR OF LIFE & LOVE

All About ME

FULL NAME :

NICKNAME

DATE OF BIRTH

LOCATION

HOSPITAL

MOTHER

FATHER

FAVORITE COLOR(S)

PERSONALITY

WEIGHT AT BIRTH

HOME ADDRESS

PHONE NUMBER

SIBLINGS

FAVORITE MEAL

BREAKFAST

LUNCH

DINNER

SNACKS

RELIGION

FAVORITE BOOK(S)/SONG(S)

Capture the Moments

Add photos or draw pictures that represent this chapter of your life.

Memories

Memories

> "LIKE BRANCHES ON A TREE, WE ALL GROW IN DIFFERENT DIRECTIONS, YET OUR ROOTS REMAIN AS ONE."
> — ANONYMOUS

A PERSONAL MEMOIR OF LIFE & LOVE

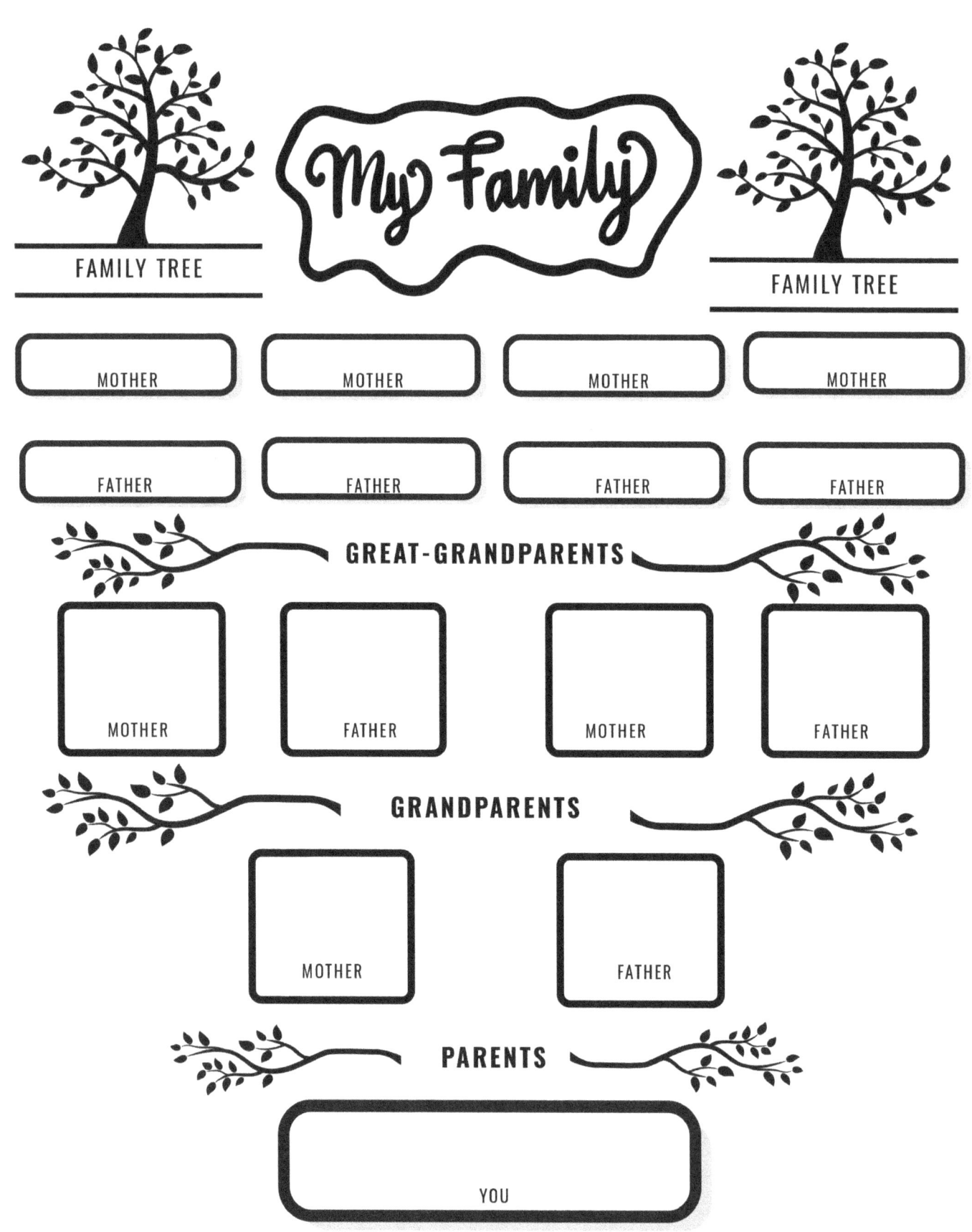

A PERSONAL MEMOIR OF LOVE & GRATITUDE

Capture the Moments

Add photos or draw pictures that represent this chapter of your life.

Memories

Memories

Memories

> "THE STORIES WE LIVE BECOME
> THE STORIES WE LEAVE BEHIND."
> — ANONYMOUS

A PERSONAL MEMOIR OF LIFE & LOVE

THE LIGHT THAT LINGERS

IDENTITY & ROOTS

A PERSONAL MEMOIR OF LOVE & LIFE

WHAT STORY DOES YOUR NAME TELL?

WHO CHOSE IT AND WHY?

WHICH FAMILY TRADITIONS SHAPED YOUR SENSE OF SELF?

DESCRIBE THE HOME YOU GREW UP IN.

WHAT DID IT LOOK, SOUND, AND SMELL LIKE?

WHAT BELIEFS FROM YOUR CHILDHOOD STILL GUIDE YOU TODAY?

HOW DID YOUR IDENTITY SHIFT BETWEEN CHILDHOOD, ADOLESCENCE, AND ADULTHOOD?

WHAT IMPACT HAS THIS HAD ON YOUR LIFE?

WHICH PLACE FELT MOST LIKE 'HOME' FOR YOU, AND WHY?

WHEN DID YOU FIRST FEEL TRULY SEEN FOR WHO YOU ARE?

WHAT PARTS OF YOUR IDENTITY HAVE BEEN MISUNDERSTOOD BY OTHERS?

WHEN YOU INTRODUCE YOURSELF, WHAT QUALITIES OF YOUR IDENTITY DO YOU INCLUDE?

additional notes

additional notes

Capture the Moments

Add photos or draw pictures that represent this chapter of your life.

Memories

Memories

"WE DO NOT REMEMBER DAYS, WE REMEMBER MOMENTS."
— CESARE PAVESE

A PERSONAL MEMOIR OF LIFE & LOVE

THE LIGHT THAT LINGERS

CHILDHOOD & COMING OF AGE

A PERSONAL MEMOIR OF LOVE & LIFE

WHAT IS YOUR EARLIEST MEMORY?

WHAT DETAILS MAKE IT VIVID?

DESCRIBE A CHILDHOOD FRIENDSHIP THAT SHAPED YOU.

WHAT DID YOU LEARN FROM IT?

WHICH ADULT (OUTSIDE YOUR FAMILY) BELIEVED IN YOU EARLY ON?

WHEN DID YOU FIRST REALIZE YOU WERE GOOD AT SOMETHING?

WHAT WERE THOSE GIFTS & TALENTS?

WRITE ABOUT A TEACHER OR CLASS THAT CHANGED YOUR PERSPECTIVE.

AS A CHILD, WHAT DID YOU WANT TO BE WHEN YOU GREW UP?

WHO OR WHAT SHAPED YOUR DECISION TO BECOME THAT?

DESCRIBE A RULE YOU BROKE AS A KID.

WHAT WAS A VALUE THAT YOU LEARNED YOUNG?

WHAT WAS A CHALLENGE THAT YOU OVERCAME?

HOW DID YOUR UPBRINGING SHAPE YOUR CHARACTER?

additional notes

additional notes

Capture the Moments

Add photos or draw pictures that represent this chapter of your life.

Memories

Memories

Memories

"OUR MOST TREASURED FAMILY HEIRLOOMS ARE OUR SWEET FAMILY MEMORIES."
— ANON

A PERSONAL MEMOIR OF LIFE & LOVE

THE LIGHT THAT LINGERS

FAMILY & RELATIONSHIPS

A PERSONAL MEMOIR OF LOVE & LIFE

HOW WOULD YOU DESCRIBE THE CULTURE OF YOUR FAMILY IN THREE SCENES?

HOW DID YOUR UPBRINGING SHAPE YOUR CHARACTER?

WHOSE LOVE LANGUAGE IN YOUR FAMILY WAS HARDEST TO READ?

HOW DID YOU LEARN IT?

DESCRIBE A TIME WHEN YOUR FAMILY PULLED TOGETHER DURING DIFFICULTY.

HOW DID THIS INSPIRE YOU TO SUPPORT OTHERS?

WHAT TRADITIONS OR ROUTINES BROUGHT YOUR FAMILY CLOSE?

WHICH TRADITIONS DO YOU VALUE THE MOST?

WHAT IMPORTANT LESSON DID AN ELDER TEACH YOU?

HOW DO YOU CARRY IT FORWARD?

WHO ARE YOUR CHOSEN FAMILY?

HOW DID THOSE BONDS FORM?

WRITE ABOUT A CONFLICT WITH SOMEONE YOU LOVE AND HOW IT CHANGED THE RELATIONSHIP.

HOW DO YOU NAVIGATE BOUNDARIES WITH RELATIVES OR FRIENDS?

WHOSE APPROVAL MATTERED MOST TO YOU?

AND HOW HAS THAT EVOLVED?

additional notes

additional notes

Capture the Moments
Add photos or draw pictures that represent this chapter of your life.

Memories

Memories

> "IN EVERY CONCEIVABLE MANNER, THE FAMILY IS THE LINK TO OUR PAST, BRIDGE TO OUR FUTURE."
> — ALEX HALEY

THE LIGHT THAT LINGERS

EDUCATION, WORK & PURPOSE

A PERSONAL MEMOIR OF LOVE & LIFE

WHAT MOMENT MADE YOU FEEL A SENSE OF CALLING OR PURPOSE?

DESCRIBE A MENTOR WHO UNLOCKED NEW POSSIBILITIES FOR YOU.

WHAT'S A RISK YOU TOOK IN SCHOOL OR WORK THAT PAID OFF?

WHEN DID YOU FEEL UNDERVALUED IN YOUR WORK?

WHAT DID YOU DO NEXT?

WHAT'S A PROJECT YOU'RE PROUD OF BECAUSE IT REFLECTS YOUR VALUES?

WHAT'S THE BEST FEEDBACK YOU EVER RECEIVED?

THE HARDEST?

HOW HAVE YOUR IDEAS OF SUCCESS CHANGED ACROSS SEASONS OF LIFE?

WRITE ABOUT A CAREER DETOUR THAT REVEALED SOMETHING ESSENTIAL.

HOW DO YOU BALANCE AMBITION, REST, AND RELATIONSHIPS?

WHERE DO YOU FEEL MOST ENERGIZED?

WHAT ARE YOU DOING, AND WITH WHOM?

WHAT ROLES HAVE YOU SERVED IN PROFESSIONALLY?

additional notes

additional notes

Capture the Moments

Add photos or draw pictures that represent this chapter of your life.

Memories

Memories

> "WE ARE SHAPED AND FASHIONED BY WHAT WE LOVE."
> — JOHANN WOLFGANG VON GOETHE

A PERSONAL MEMOIR OF LIFE & LOVE

THE LIGHT THAT LINGERS

HOME, PLACES & BELONGING

A PERSONAL MEMOIR OF LOVE & LIFE

WHAT CITY OR LANDSCAPE HAS SHAPED YOUR WORLDVIEW THE MOST?

WHERE DO YOU GO WHEN YOU NEED TO THINK CLEARLY?

WHAT DOES YOUR IDEAL HOME FEEL LIKE?

WHAT VALUES DOES IT EXPRESS?

WRITE ABOUT A JOURNEY THAT CHANGED YOUR SENSE OF HOME.

HOW HAS MOVING (OR STAYING PUT) FORMED YOU?

WHEN HAVE YOU FELT LIKE AN OUTSIDER?

AND WHAT HELPED YOU BELONG?

WHAT MAP WOULD TELL THE STORY OF YOUR LIFE?

WHAT STOPS ARE ESSENTIAL?

HOW DO YOU CREATE A SENSE OF SANCTUARY FOR YOURSELF?

additional notes

additional notes

Capture the Moments

Add photos or draw pictures that represent this chapter of your life.

Memories

Memories

> "IT IS NOT LENGTH OF LIFE, BUT DEPTH OF LIFE."
> — RALPH WALDO EMERSON

A PERSONAL MEMOIR OF LIFE & LOVE

THE LIGHT THAT LINGERS

TRADITION, CULTURE & CELEBRATIONS

A PERSONAL MEMOIR OF LOVE & LIFE

WHICH HOLIDAY OR TRADITION BEST REFLECTS YOUR HERITAGE?

WHY?

WHAT IS A TRADITION YOU STARTED ON YOUR OWN?

WHY?

DESCRIBE A RECIPE THAT CARRIES A FAMILY STORY.

HOW DO YOU HONOR THOSE WHO CAME BEFORE YOU?

WHY?

WHICH OBJECT (HEIRLOOM OR NOT) HOLDS CULTURAL MEANING FOR YOU?

WHY?

WHAT CULTURAL MISUNDERSTANDING DID YOU LIVE THROUGH AND LEARN FROM?

WHAT ROLE DOES HUMOR PLAY IN YOUR FAMILY OR CULTURE?

HOW DO YOU WANT TO EVOLVE THE TRADITIONS YOU INHERITED?

additional notes

additional notes

Capture the Moments

Add photos or draw pictures that represent this chapter of your life.

Memories

Memories

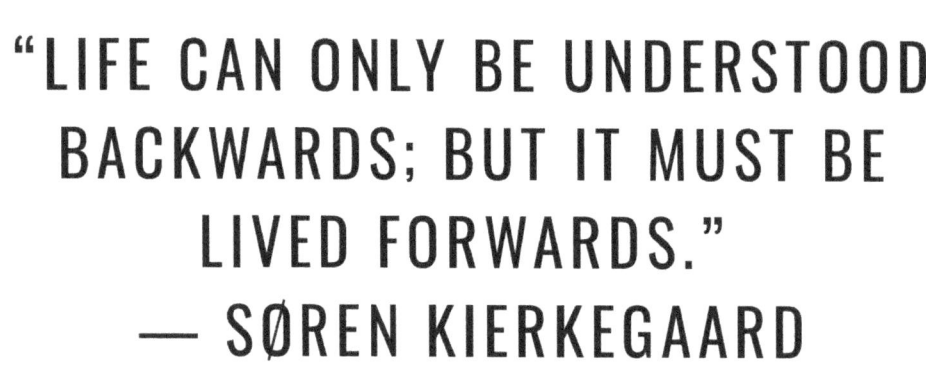

"LIFE CAN ONLY BE UNDERSTOOD BACKWARDS; BUT IT MUST BE LIVED FORWARDS."
— SØREN KIERKEGAARD

A PERSONAL MEMOIR OF LIFE & LOVE

THE LIGHT THAT LINGERS

CHALLENGES & RESILIENCE

A PERSONAL MEMOIR OF LOVE & LIFE

WRITE ABOUT A SETBACK THAT TAUGHT YOU RESILIENCE.

_____
_____
_____
_____
_____
_____
_____
_____
_____

WHAT IS A FEAR YOU FACED HEAD-ON?

_____
_____
_____
_____
_____
_____
_____
_____
_____
_____

WHEN DID YOU ASK FOR HELP—AND WHAT MADE IT POSSIBLE?

DESCRIBE A TIME YOU HAD TO START OVER.

HOW DID YOU BEGIN?

HOW DO YOU PROCESS LOSS OR DISAPPOINTMENT?

WHAT COPING STRATEGIES SERVE YOU?

WHICH ONES NO LONGER DO?

WHEN DID YOU CHOOSE COURAGE OVER COMFORT?

WHAT BOUNDARY DID YOU SET THAT PROTECTED YOUR WELL-BEING?

HOW DID YOU REBUILD TRUST AFTER IT WAS BROKEN?

WHAT PERSONAL MYTH DID YOU LET GO OF TO GROW?

additional notes

additional notes

Capture the Moments

Add photos or draw pictures that represent this chapter of your life.

Memories

Memories

> "THE MEANING OF LIFE IS TO FIND YOUR GIFT. THE PURPOSE OF LIFE IS TO GIVE IT AWAY."
> — PABLO PICASSO

THE LIGHT THAT LINGERS

JOY, PASSIONS & HOBBIES

A PERSONAL MEMOIR OF LOVE & LIFE

WHAT ACTIVITY MAKES YOU LOSE TRACK OF TIME?

_____
_____
_____
_____
_____
_____
_____
_____

DESCRIBE A COLLECTION, HOBBY, OR CRAFT THAT BRINGS YOU JOY.

_____
_____
_____
_____
_____
_____
_____
_____

WHICH BOOK, FILM, OR SONG CHANGED YOUR MOOD OR MIND RECENTLY?

WHAT'S A SMALL DAILY PLEASURE YOU PROTECT FIERCELY?

WHEN DO YOU LAUGH THE HARDEST?

WITH WHOM?

WHAT HAVE YOU CREATED THAT YOU'RE PROUD OF?

HOW DO YOU RECHARGE AFTER A DRAINING DAY?

_____
_____
_____
_____
_____
_____
_____
_____
_____

WHERE DO YOU FIND BEAUTY MOST EASILY?

_____
_____
_____
_____
_____
_____
_____
_____
_____

WHAT DREAM TRIP OR EXPERIENCE IS STILL ON YOUR LIST—WHY?

additional notes

additional notes

Capture the Moments

Add photos or draw pictures that represent this chapter of your life.

Memories

Memories

> "THE GREATEST USE OF LIFE IS TO SPEND IT FOR SOMETHING THAT WILL OUTLAST IT."
> — WILLIAM JAMES

THE LIGHT THAT LINGERS

FAITH, VALUES & PHILOSOPHY

A PERSONAL MEMOIR OF LOVE & LIFE

WHICH VALUES ANCHOR YOUR DECISIONS WHEN LIFE GETS COMPLICATED?

HOW HAS YOUR FAITH OR PHILOSOPHY EVOLVED OVER TIME?

WHAT TRADITIONS HELP YOU MARK BEGINNINGS AND ENDINGS?

WHEN DID YOU ACT AGAINST YOUR VALUES, AND WHAT DID YOU LEARN?

HOW DO YOU PRACTICE GRATITUDE?

DESCRIBE A MORAL DILEMMA YOU WORKED THROUGH HONESTLY.

WHAT DOES FORGIVENESS LOOK LIKE IN YOUR LIFE—GIVING AND RECEIVING?

HOW DO YOU DEFINE INTEGRITY FOR YOURSELF?

WHAT WISDOM WOULD YOU WRITE TO YOUR YOUNGER SELF?

additional notes

additional notes

Capture the Moments

Add photos or draw pictures that represent this chapter of your life.

Memories

Memories

Memories

> "THE GREATEST THING YOU'LL EVER LEARN IS JUST TO LOVE AND BE LOVED IN RETURN."
> — EDEN AHBEZ

THE LIGHT THAT LINGERS

LEGACY & HOPES

A PERSONAL MEMOIR OF LOVE & LIFE

WHAT DO YOU WANT TO BE REMEMBERED FOR?

BY WHOM?

WHAT STORIES DO YOU HOPE FUTURE GENERATIONS WILL TELL ABOUT YOU?

IF YOUR LIFE HAD A MOTTO, WHAT WOULD IT BE?

HOW DO YOU WANT YOUR COMMUNITY TO BE DIFFERENT BECAUSE YOU WERE HERE?

WRITE A BLESSING FOR THE PEOPLE YOU LOVE.

WHAT LESSONS TOOK THE LONGEST TO LEARN —AND ARE WORTH PASSING ON?

WHAT ARTIFACTS OF YOUR LIFE SHOULD BE KEPT AND WHY?

WHAT DO YOU HOPE THE NEXT CHAPTER OF YOUR LIFE HOLDS?

HOW WILL YOU MEASURE A LIFE WELL-LIVED?

additional notes

additional notes

Capture the Moments

Add photos or draw pictures that represent this chapter of your life.

Memories

Memories

> "OWNING OUR STORY AND LOVING OURSELVES THROUGH THAT PROCESS IS THE BRAVEST THING WE'LL EVER DO."
> — BRENÉ BROWN

Life's *Reflections*

(Overview)
SUMMARIZE KEY EVENTS

(Achievements)
WHAT WERE YOUR MAJOR ACHIEVEMENTS?

(Gratitude)
LIST THREE THINGS YOU'RE MOST GRATEFUL FOR.

(Priorities)
IDENTIFY KEY PRIORITIES AND GOALS.

○ _____
○ _____
○ _____
○ _____
○ _____

A PERSONAL MEMOIR OF LIFE & LOVE

Dear _____,

LETTER TO LOVED ONE

WITH LOVE,

*D*EAR LETTER TO LOVED ONE

_____ ,

WITH LOVE,

_____

DEAR _____,
LETTER TO LOVED ONE

WITH LOVE,

_____

*D*EAR LETTER TO LOVED ONE

_____ ,

WITH LOVE,

_____

Dear _____,

LETTER TO LOVED ONE

WITH LOVE,

_____

Capture the Moments

Add photos or draw pictures that represent this chapter of your life.

Memories

Memories

Capture the Moments

Add photos or draw pictures that represent this chapter of your life.

Memories

Memories

> "YOUR STORY IS WHAT YOU HAVE, WHAT YOU WILL ALWAYS HAVE. IT IS SOMETHING TO OWN."
> — MICHELLE OBAMA

ADDITIONAL MEMOIR PUBLICATIONS

ROOTED IN YOU
A CHILD'S MEMOIR OF LOVE AND GRATITUDE

CARRIED IN MY HEART
A MOTHER'S MEMOIR OF LOVE AND LEGACY

GUIDED BY MY HANDS
A FATHER'S MEMOIR OF LOVE AND STRENGTH

BOUND BY OUR VOWS
A SPOUSE'S MEMOIR OF LOVE AND DEVOTION

FOR MORE INFORMATION OR
TO PURCHASE ADDITIONAL COPIES
WWW.ATOSHALOGAN.COM

Every life tells a story...

Through moments of triumph and heartbreak, struggle and renewal, this memoir invites you to walk alongside the author on a deeply personal journey. From roots that ground us to branches reaching toward new beginnings, these pages reflect on the lessons of the past and the promise of tomorrow.

More than a record of one life, this memoir is an invitation to reflect on your own story. It is a reminder that while we cannot choose every circumstance, we can choose the legacy we leave behind.

Whether you are seeking encouragement, reflection, or simply a heartfelt story, this book offers something to carry with you. May it inspire you to embrace your own journey with gratitude, courage, and love.

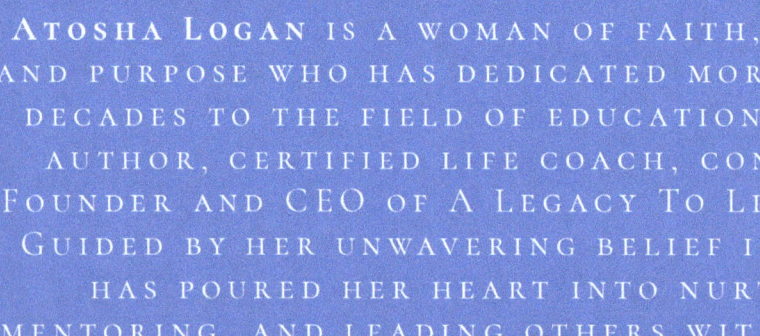

Atosha Logan is a woman of faith, strength, and purpose who has dedicated more than two decades to the field of education and is an author, certified life coach, consultant, Founder and CEO of A Legacy To Live For Inc. Guided by her unwavering belief in God, she has poured her heart into nurturing, mentoring, and leading others with integrity and personal motivation. Her journey reflects resilience, hope, and a deep commitment to uplifting and empowering others.

www.ingramcontent.com/pod-product-compliance
Lightning Source LLC
Chambersburg PA
CBHW081359070526
44583CB00020B/2592